STORY

of

HAPPINESS

Prose and Songs

KERRY SUSAN DRAKE

To order additional copies of this book, contact:
Xlibris
AU TFN: 1 800 844 927 (Toll Free inside Australia)
AU Local: 0283 108 187 (+61 2 8310 8187 from outside Australia)
www.xlibris.com.au
Orders@Xlibris.com.au

ISBN: Softcover   978-1-6641-0202-6
        Hardcover   978-1-6641-0203-3
        EBook   978-1-6641-0201-9

Print information available on the last page

Rev. date: 05/04/2022

CONTENTS

Talking to God

Talking to God, talking to the higher authority.

Back in 2009 I was considering my lonliness and talking to God about sending an Angel into my life. I was in the attitude of discussing with the Higher Power, God the Father if He could provide me with a friendship/relationship. I exorted talking with God for at least 30 minutes as I lay in my bed. I knew I had joined a dating club LDS MINGLE.

And I knew that if I believed God was listening He would answer me with a suitable LDS partner, an Angel.

I had been divorced for 7 years and had many bad boyfriends who were not LDS.

I knew there had to be someone and I built my faith on prayer.

I woke the next morning to find on LDSMINGLE a true interested angel.

I knew that He would be temporary but indeed here on the screen was my potential partner. The story of Happiness began for me. He was a true friend and fulfilled my need. As James the Apostle says "if any of you lack wisdom? Ask of God".

We courted for 9 months my soon to be partner via skype, and he visited downunder to meet me twice. What followed was engagement and then finally marriage civily in Dubuque USA with his family.

My angel stayed with me for 10 years and I was so blessed by the partnership. He was so mature and understanding of my first marriage and got to know my ex, and in the process of getting to know my 3 children who were adults made every attempt to be accepted. Our divorce came as a realisation that my first family was the priority.

I feel and acknowledge he was sent as an angel in answer to prayer. Asking and receiving.

I believe in Prayer is a song I wrote about this and is on ldsradiostation.com.

Story of Happiness (A true story using fictional names)

The story of happiness began one day in May. Doctor Paul Anderson had a full quota of needy clients to help that day the first of May.

As a doctor of general practice his clients ranged from the young to the very old. And his oldest client was a very fitly gentlemen aged ninety.

Harry the ninety-year old had an appointment that day the first of May. Doctor Paul, was indeed aware of Harold's situation because of the many years of being the family doctor.

Sitting in the waiting room Harry had a lot to feel weary and unwell about in life now. Although his life was not entirely miserable as he knew that his lovely wife Rose who had passed away in April he could never replace. Greif and loss surrounded his awkward life now without a wife.

What he knew is that he missed Rose a tremendous lot and his sorrow for her loss meant a loss of happiness.

When Doctor Paul called him into his room for a consultation. Harry sat down and told of his loss and grief.

"Rose my life has departed this mortal life and I am alone. What can I do Doctor Paul?" asked Harry in a pleading tone of fear, approbation and shear despair.

Doctor Paul looking at Harry knew his ability to help would be up to the Lord, being a Christian and ofcourse discussing life after death was a topic Harry could handle.

Talking with Harry, Doctor Paul issued Harry a prescription; the usual Harry needed for this loss. And said "the tide has come in but it will go out and I am sure your wife wants happiness for you".

Harry kept his company now with a dog named Suzie and a cat named Princess. They cheered him and smothered him at the same time. But it was not like having a wife.

Harry left the clinic that day with a prescription but what was to happen next was Doctor Paul was to meet with Madeline a 85 years senior and told quite the same story of grief and loss.

Doctor Paul's client Madeline in a very unwell state revealed to her doctor; "I am so unhappy my dear beloved Ralf, husband and companion has gone to God" Madeline remarked.

In solemnity I miss Ralf so much and I am in a state of never ending depression was her cry.

Doctor Paul did give her the same medicine and said come back in a weeks time.

Doctor Paul had a mission he could see to put Harry in contact with Madeline.

Knowing instinctively that companion ship and ministering to Harry and Madeline was a reassuring reminder to Dr Paul; 'It is not good for man to be alone'.

The secret to his own life of happiness was truely a wife. And Mrs Anderson was indeed the backbone of his strength to go on.

Harry and Madeline must meet each other was the remedy Dr Paul knew can bring them happiness.

Doctor Paul actively spoke to his secretary and got her to send for Harry to visit the clinic to tell him about Madeline.

The course of life would and could be fulfilled if Harry met Madeline. They could share there story's and help each other.

It was a chance for a little romance.

Such was the day when Doctor Paul sat with Harry in his suite. He promptly told Harry about Madeline his client.

Doctor Paul asked Harry for permission to give Madeline his phone number. And vice versa Madeline was asked permission to have her phone number to give Harry.

The mutual appreciation of both was not dismissed. And what happened next is a story of happiness. Harry did ring Madeline. He did ask her about having a lemon tea with him.

Doctor Paul somehow knew their meeting and sharing their own grief and loss would somehow comfort them.

In actual reality Harry took Madeline out often. He took her to the musical Funny Girl, and the next musical at the Whitehorse Centre Thoroughly Modern Millie.

This was such happiness. Harry was 90 and Madeline was 85. Seniors having the time of their lives.

I the author of this tale was sitting next to Harry the day of the musical and I asked Harry who was 90. "What is the secret to your longevity?" and he amazingly replied...

I have a new life, and new wife. I eat 9 biscuits a day and that's not all. I enjoy a walk."

Such was the joy of his life, that Doctor Paul and his foresight to put this couple intouch with each other.

It was my delight to hear this. How miracles are performed by the doctors of today. And we need more of them. Amen.

A Prayer Saved My Life

A Prayer saved my life, is what marked my recovery from falling off a galloping horse.

It was at the age of 18 years young. I was invited with friends to go on a horse riding activity. All my friends from work who were laboratory workers. And I was an Animal Technician at The Walter and Eliza Hall institute of Medical Research. Yes! i was fulfilling my ambitions at the time after qualifying in Applied Science at Northcote Technical College.

On the Saturday in April I ventured to go with my friend's horse riding at Broaford a small country town off Sydney Road.

It was pleasant weather and just right for outdoors roaming. And I had no anxiety as it was a casual riding day and the horses on the ranch were well trained in the route to go.

I had this feeling I was safe and I noticed that my horse was slower than the others. Infact I felt at the time I was too far behind in the stream of horses as my friends were so far ahead of my horse riding.

Quickly i thought at the time 'I must catch up'.

This was the beginning of me kicking the horse to get to a gallop. It was not a good move.

The horse would not respond but as I persisted the horse did get moving quicker and unbe known to me my lack of experience found me dumbly choosing to gallop as I rode the horse 'crash' is all i knew when my body was on the ground, my right side of the head and body hit the ground and I was burdened by the pain that went through my ride of the body from head to toe.

I was alive but I could not exert any conscious reaction. I lay on the ground in shock.

And my friend who I cannot recall her name was crying beside me.

I felt enormous awareness of her weeping. And then I began to cry out to 'GOD'.

I said 'dear God help me. Please don't let me have any broken bones?'

I was so still on the ground I felt a peace come over me. My friend was still crying and alarmed all the other riders.

I then began to feel in those unconscious seconds, I woke up out of the shock and got to my full stature and went to sit on a log.

The horse and my crying friend were staring at me, and the most profound act of God happened. The horse came over to me and kissed me on the cheek!

I was in more shock!

But I was revived although I could not utter any words to my friend.

I knew that the power of prayer had made the difference. I could have been profoundly unable to walk back with the horse to the ranch, but I did slowly with me friend walk beside the horse and made it back home that day.

To make an appointment with a doctor to assess any issues, from the fall off the horse.

My fall was reported to my supervising doctor at Walter and Eliza Hall Institute. Doctor Holmes sent me to the adjacent hospital Royal Melbourne for a thorough xrays from head to toe.

I was fortunate I had a jarred pelvis and that was all.

I worked for Doctor Moore in research of cancer, on the sixth floor in a certain breed of mice. So, I was in a responsible role.

A prayer saved my life. And the power of prayer led me to realising my Christian faith.

As I recalled my healing is what lead me to investigate The Church of Jesus Christ of Latter-Day Saints at age 19.

My time of recovery was a small miracle. As I could have become a quadriplegic or affected with brain damage.

Thus, I am a very grateful Christian since 1974, and can still acknowledge Prayer as a Life Saver.

Healing By Faith

My faith healing happened as I was in church during a sacrament meeting.

I was stricken with a heavy cold. I was sitting at the back of the hall away from parishoner's.

I was feeling low but somehow felt resolute in faith to be healed.

The sacrament meeting was underway with the procedures of passing of the sacrament bread and water. And the first two spiritual talks.

The intermediate hymn was 'The Spirit Of God" and the lyrics followed as the congregation sang with great temper, 'like a fire is burning'; my spirit was so boyed that I felt so invigorated and strengthened. I felt a tremendous zeal and I suddenly knew my spirit was so strong.

The blanket of depressing flu left my body. So as like a heavy blanket it was lifted off.

I suddenly became aware that my heavy cold and the weakness was gone.

The Spirit of God like a fire burned so that the epiphany of a spiritual miracle had occured.

I was healed in a moment of great faith stirring miracle and I knew that it was a blessing.

Hallelujah, God had performed thru me a faith healing.

God Answered

The heavens were opened to me. On two occasions I was financially in a pickle.

I had applied for a grant of financial benefit for my community theatre, but was rejected.

I sought the Lord in prayer talking out loud my concerns at night pleading for help.

My prayers were long and full of emotion.

The first instance of Gods goodness was realised when I found in my bank account with extra money the next day, unknown to me thousands had been transferred. I was so relieved and blessed and I knew this blessing was God answering my prayer.

The other occasion was when I was indebt due to not gaining a grant to cover theatre expenses.

I pleaded once more to God the Father for help. The miracle of faith was I became redundant from my position as a Telephone Interviewer. Yes and the years I had worked for AC Nielson added up to a redundancy package that entirely paid off my thousands in debt. And i had two new jobs to go to.

I was so grateful instead of fearful. God answered in away that blessed me doubly.

It was a miracle and my faith was so strengthened.

A Miracle from the Spirit World

This is about an extraordinary gift from the spirit world.

I had two sets of 6 crystal glasses in separate boxes. I did not realise the fragility of these glasses and after using a glass filled with a refreshment of cold chocolate milk. I found out how fragile crystal glass is.

I washed it with hot water and it imploded. And I was left with 11 crystal glasses. It was my thought I'll never be able to replace it.

I was a private teacher and nanny and the job came to an end and the flat I was living in was to be demolished.

I rang Catholic Homes to tell them of my need for accommodation urgently.

I was able to get accommodation and it was a huge relief. Though this was a blessing. It wasn't till being moved in and I still had 11 crystal glasses. I was into getting to know the neighbours and inviting them to lunch, and it was a miracle in that moment of cleaning my crystal glasses. A crystal glass popped into my sink. How did I know this was the 12th glass arriving from the spirit world. Because it did not have a label it was crystal clear and I counted. Whow! This was a miracle. My faith was so strengthened by the Goodness of God.

I thank God in my prayers for all my blessings I know have come direct from Faith and being a practicing Christian.

I strive for morality and honesty and acknowledge the Heavens and the unseen world of nature.

Story of Eve

EVE I ask myself why am I writing about EVE?…the mother of all living the woman taken out of man. A leader in no uncertain terms. To start the human race. Who brought humanity, mortality into the world. Who made the choice and accepted the responsibility to go and announce to Adam; I have partaken of the fruit of the Tree of knowledge of Good and Evil!

This powerful step brought her mortality and separated her distinctly from Adam. Adam had known the commandment not to partake and did not partake when offered the fruit of the Tree. The serpent he did not accept as authorised. Of course, Adam and Eve walked and talked with God and Jesus.

Eve took the initiative and was obedient to God the Father knowing that this decision brought death and a knowledge of Good and Evil to her. Decisions had to be made and her first decision was to partake of the fruit that was delicious recognising that making her leadership role accountable. Eve and desire to multiply and replenish the earth was a powerful step in the direction of Good.

Remembering also the commandment given. Eve took it unto herself to start knowing how delicious to the taste was the fruit accepting the temptation informally and beginning an accountability for mortality. Taken out of the side of man Eve being the Rib…became woman and the literal connection as wo…woo… love of man.

Eve announces her leadership role and capitalises on her journey now in mortality and invites Adam to partake of mortality. The reckoning is a vital path of change and dropping out of a spiritual world, an innocent world, a calmer life with God the Father and Jesus His son.

The cost to her Eve is that of not being alone. The casting out and relying on Adam to agree to a plan that would involve a seeking of a redeemer…even that of Jesus Christ for the atonement.

No greater decision has ever been known but that of Eve doing what was blindly a misleading attempt by Satan the Serpent to control her and destabilise her mission.

Eve was a missionary, a great and is a great leader of Women now and always. Constantly reminding us that her fame is put under question and intimidated as having made the Bad come into the world. No! stop it was Satan and the Serpent who deliberately put Eve in a diabolical risk. Eve triumphed out of the misery and so her strength inline with Adam her husband was united and bonded in eternal love.

Such is the Story of Eve.

EVE was a beautiful spirit of intelligence made perfect in the eyes of Adam. Her majesty and character are recognised and can never be underestimated being the first Mother of mortals. We are indebted to her mission and the gateway opened this brave and most precious life it gives to all spirits. I honour and feel incredibly grateful Eve gave her life and mortal announcement with grace and received forgiveness with Grace.

We live in a fullness of time, with freedom to choose the fruit to partake of Good and Evil. The knowledge that each has outcomes, consequences.

To choose the Tree of Life of eternal life would not be fair to take mistakes with us. A Redeemer offers us a path to reconciliation.

Eve knowing of her mission chose the Right, as we accept that her marriage was existent…the mere decision to uphold the plan is that some do not know of this. Innocently denoting Eve as a fallen woman is never written in the Holy Word of God.

Thus, legitimacy of her noble act was indeed a small but significant deposition. An act of love. An act of obedience to the Father of spirits going forward. Obeying the commandment. Perhaps listening to the Serpent was as innocent in the beguiling that serpent had mastery of. But love is a higher motivation. A more courageous act. Eve knowing her true Master makes us aware in mortality we are challenged. Eve was vulnerable without Adam.

God the Father sees the anguish of His children Adam and Eve. Giving strength and faith to them to seek Jesus their Redeemer, as a friend, as a brother to guide them in mortality.

Eve settles into her new role and knows that with Adam and Jesus. Peace will acquiesce.

The Story of Eve.

Bruce R. McConkie wrote in 1966…Scant knowledge is available to us of Eve (the wife of Adam) and her achievements in pre-existence and in mortality. Without question she was like unto her mighty husband Adam in, intelligence and in devotion to righteousness, during both her first and second estates of existence.

She was placed on earth in the same manner as was Adam, the Mosaic account of the Lord creating her from Adam's rib being merely figurative. (Moses 3. 20-25)

Eve was the first woman; she became the mother of the whole human race, her very name signifying "mother of all living". (Moses 4:26; 1 Ne 5:11.) Strictly speaking it was she who partook of the forbidden fruit, with the resultant change in the physical body from a state of immortality to mortality. Adam thereafter partook in order to comply with the command to multiply and fill the earth with posterity. "Adam was not deceived, but the woman being deceived was in the transgression." (1Tim. 2:14.)

Before the fall Eve was sealed to Adam in the new and everlasting covenant of marriage, a ceremony performed by the Lord before death entered the world and therefore one destined to last forever. (Moses 3:20-25.) After the fall the Lord said to her: "I will greatly multiply thy sorrow and thy conception. In sorrow thou shalt bring forth children, and thy desire shall be to thy husband, and he shall rule over thee." (Moses 4 : 22.)

One of the perfect summaries of the plan of salvation ever given fell from the lips of Eve: Were it not for our transgression," she said "we should never have had seed and never should have known good and evil, and the joy of our redemption, and the eternal life which God giveth unto all the obedient." (Moses 5:11.) Indeed, Eve is a participant with Adam in all his ministry, and will inherit jointly with him all the blessings appertaining to his high state of exaltation.

Eve had a calling beside Adam. They were leaders, Eve was equal and truly one with Adam. We can speculate the maturity of Eve was challenged supposing her to be under threat by Satan being alone Eve sought to obey all of God's commandments. And being wise to make judgements her first desire was to progress making a process possible. Against the law not to partake of the forbidden fruit…Eve in innocence does what must be the most well-known error in all history…an error that can only be undone and understood by God the Father and His Son Jesus. Who gave Adam specific teachings with the right to choose. If Eve had not disobeyed this option secretly given; the opportunity of advancement still would have been approved and consequently and unequivocally been a righteous decision between God and Adam and Eve.

The role of Satan least understood has him vying for control, never offering console. Telling about good and Evil in its context. Eve is beguiled. Not having known before that her brother was interfering and seeking his own authority over her.

Eve faces her enemy. And then seeks Adam and this is the finest of all relationships. Wherein both know they must face God naked having learnt opposing values; the good that they had to talk with God and the humiliating fact of disobeying God.

It's a fact Adam tells God the Father, 'the woman thou gavest me did eat the forbidden fruit, and I did eat also" the surrender of guilt that is not mine…perhaps is compassionately seen as Adam's tripping to Eve but staying together was more important and keeping to the plan of salvation. Serves to save with issues that do follow their future lives together.

According to the King James Version, The Holy Bible "And I will put enmity between thee and the woman, and between thy seed and her seed: it shall bruise thy head, and thou bruise his heel. (Gen 3: 15.) Eve has an emotionally intelligent grasp that would be tested with opposition and enmity. While it can harm Eve or the living it would be in her head the Fall. And yet be a crown that would bruise his heel. Literally stop the man from progressing. So, Eve could not do anything that would not affect the whole relationship. Emotion would make the psychology of Eve as a diabolical and integral partner to Adam. And so, woman is as much a power to behold. Adam was her in the beginning when asleep for out of him came his first wife.

Eve's children recorded are Awan (daughter); Cain (son); Azura (daughter); Abel (son); Seth (son); Aclima (daughter).

Eve did have daughters and sons and they are well known for their spirituality.

The spirituality is a sensitive subject when discussing the outcomes of her children's lives; as they do capture the enormous world of survival they had to bear. It tells of the way in which God moved among them and so did the adversity of Satan or Lucifer. When death came into the world with the first murder…Cain slays his brother Abel.

Eve rescues the family by bearing Seth after Cain being cast out, cursed and sent to dwell outside. Cain was sent far away.

Herbert Lockyer in 1967 wrote Eve was the first woman to be called a wife. Fashioned out of man, she became man's counterpart and companion. God saw that although Adam was in a state of perfect innocency, it was not good for him to be alone.. It would be good for him spiritually, intellectually and socially to have a wife. He needed someone to love and bear his children since the command had gone forth "to multiply and replenish the earth", and so with Adam-

The world was sad, the garden was a wild. And the man a hermit sighed till woman smiled.

God spoke of the woman He was to provide for Adam as his "helpmeet" – a helpmeet or adapted to him – a term giving woman her true position in the world. It is only where the Bible exists and Christianity is practiced that she attains to such a position as the helper, or equal of man. In lands where darkness reigns, woman is the slave, the chattel of man. Thus, Eve was given to Adam and their two hearts beat as one in love for each other and for God. Eve was formed while Adam slept. He knew no pain during the operation for as yet there was no sin in the world.

How true it is that God is continually working while men sleep! He often imparts real blessings to His own as they sleep (Psalm 127:2.)

When I wake from sleep,

Despair has fled and hope is near;

The sky seems blue, and visions clear

Have banished all my dread and fear.

Eve: Bible Jewish Women's Archive it is said Who was the first woman in the Bible?

Lilith

According to the "first Eve" story Lilith

Was created by God from dust and placed to live in the garden with Adam until problems arose between Adam and Lilith when Adam tried to exercise dominance over Lilith.

Again The History of Lilith – Blood, Gender and Power in Christianity and Judaism. We are told Lilith is an extremely controversial figure within Jewish Folklore. Lilith's name is not included in the creation story of the Torah but she appears in several midrashic texts.

Her symbolism, history and literature are debated among Jewish scholars, feminists and other intellectuals. There are multiple origin stories for Lilith as the first wife of Adam. According to the "first Eve" story Lilith was created by God from dust and placed to live in the garden with Adam until problems arose between Adam and Lilith when Adam tried to exercise dominance over Lilith.

One story tells that Lilith refused to lay beneath Adam during sex. She believed they were created equal, both from the dust of the earth, thus she should not have to lay beneath him. After Adam disagreed, Lilith fled the Garden of Eden to gain her independence. Adam told God that Lilith had left and God sent three angels, Senoi, Sansenoi, and Sammangelof, to retrieve her. The three angels found Lilith in a cave bearing children, but Lilith refused to come back to the garden. The angels told her they would kill 100 of her children every day for her disobedience. In revenge, she is said to rob children life and is responsible for the deaths of still-born infants and crib deaths (SIDS). Male children are at risk of Lilith's wrath for 8 days after birth (until circumcision) and girls are at risk for 20 days. Although Lilith stole children's lives in the night, she agreed not to kill the children who had amulets of either of the three angels.

After the angels' departure, Lilith tried to return to the garden but upon her arrival she discovered that Adam already had another mate, Eve. Out of revenge, Lilith had sex with Adam while he was sleeping and "stole his seed." With his seed she bears 'Lilium,' earth-bound demons to replace her children killed by the angels. Lilith is also said to be responsible for males erotic dreams and night emissions.

Another theory says that Lilith is impregnated, thus creating more demons by masturbation and erotic dreams.

The History of Lilith

Although the figure of Lilith is commonly found in Jewish folklore and midrash, the origin of Lilith is as a Sumarian succubus. The first Jewish story of Lilith was told in the Alphabet of ben sirah. Before the introduction of the Alphabet of ben sirah, Lilith was mostly seen as a demoness instead of the "first Eve". https://www2kenyon.edu : Rein91

Folklore is mythology and to understand the nature of this fictitious tale we need to go to other sources.

Chapter Two

Adam and Eve in Mormonism

The Church of Jesus Christ of Latter-day Saints (LDS Church) teaches that Adam and Eve were the first man and the first woman to live on the earth and that their fall was an essential step in the plan of salvation. Adam in particular is a central figure in Mormon cosmology. Robert L. Miller, a Latter-day Saint author wrote of the church's perspective:

Few persons in all eternity have been more directly involved in the plan of salvation-the creation, the fall, and the ultimate redemption of the children of God—than the man Adam. His ministry among the sons and daughters of earth stretches from the distant past of pre-mortality to the distant future of resurrection, judgement and beyond.

Identity of Adam and Eve

According to LDS Church teachings, all people on the earth lived with God the Father and Jesus Christ in a premortal life. Adam and Eve were "among our Father's noblest children" and they were "foreordained" to be the parents of the human race. In the pre-mortal life, Adam was the archangel, Michael.

Why am I writing about Eve? It is because to me I see her as a woman of great faith. A High Priestess, one who is noble and beautiful. And from her the "mother of all living" I believe I eventually came to earth. After the many generations of spirits. I agreed with her role and waited for my time to be born of goodly parents. To build up the Kingdom of God on earth.

I share with you now other women's comments about Eve.

MY THOUGHTS ABOUT EVE, THE FIRST WOMAN ON EARTH by Gail Hellings

I'd been asked by Susan Kerry Drake for my thoughts about Eve. This is what I wrote early 2022 –

So, what did I know about Eve at all?

This was the first time I'd really investigated my own thoughts about her and I was surprised by them, things that I'd never considered before in regard to her, became evident in my mind.

I'd really never bothered to think about Eve other than read what is told of her in the bible, however upon being asked for my thoughts, I had a new experience. In the process of having to put my thoughts on paper, I discovered startling new ideas.

I found that in writing about her, there came a new admiration and respect for her as well as a "hit me like a brick" realization that SHE, not Adam, was THE FIRST at so many things of importance. She was THE FIRST PERSON in the entire history of the world to make a decision between two choices. One single decision that was vital. One single decision that began the history of mankind. So this is what I wrote –

Eve, the first woman to live upon the Earth, was placed in a position where she had to make a choice between two things.

It's the first choice made by anyone in recorded history that would settle the outcome of this world and it's purpose, and so she was the first person ever to be placed in that situation. She had no-one to discuss her decision with, no one to advise her.

Eve judged for herself, using her limited understanding and having had no earlier experience with weighing up each matter or judging the consequences, she then made the decision we know she made.

I'm happy with the decision she made.

She later went through childbirth without anyone to help her other than her untrained husband.

She raised a family without any others to get advice from. She'd never experienced childhood herself and so had no experience in any matter concerning the raising of children or anything else she would need to know during her life. She had no mother to ask advice from; no Aunts, no uncles, no women friends and thus she pioneered the way herself, for others who would live on the earth with her.

She experienced disharmony and tragedy within her own family with no-one to turn to but God and her husband for consolation.

There were no toilets, taps, washing machines or shops. Everything had to be grown, built, dug, made and fetched by Eve and her husband Adam.

While many see her only as the person who brought sin into the world, a woman who succumb

Bed to the enticing of the devil, I don't see her that way.

She was a pioneer in all things and an example to me.

Gail Hellings

Eve wanted to live in a paradise earth.

She was told if she ate the apple something would happen.
Eve had a bit of snake in her.
Maybe there is a lesson we learn from Adam and Eve.
They both didn't listen to God.
And they both partook of the fruit.
Satan came and tested them.
And that's when the wars started-

Cheryl Drake

It's the original story.

Penelope Amaudruz

Eve was brave, courageous and noble. A woman of faith. And a daughter of the Father God.

We know that Eve lived for somewhat 900 years and saw the generations of man. Eve did an everlasting life of service and leading the way for sons and daughters of the Most High God.

We are indebted to her example and the hope given to all the generations that came because of Eve's tribute to motherhood.

A divine role and calling.

It is an original story and the Bible gives us a caption in writing of the detail available from Moses.

It was a dynasty. A remarkably historical written document – a translation in poetic verse. The New King James Version is best allegory- a part of the story that can be interpreted. It is a remarkable story. Eve was able to give as much as Adam being a creation and person of high worth.

I ask myself why does the Bible give us the contrast of good and evil? And I feel it is the fact that a Saviour was needed in this life for those who went otherwise of God's commandments.

It is necessary we are redeemed. Giving us all the path to change.

The contrast would Eve witness in the family and the future generations as a result of her decision and Adam's decision to ask God for a solution came with the looking forward to a Saviour Jesus Christ.

Why the tree of knowledge of Good and Evil is in the Garden of Eden is a metaphor for choice.

The Tree of Life is the sweet, righteous fruit of peace. And we know peace is a part of the plan.

WE taste of the bitter and sweet or sweet and bitter because we have freedom to believe or doubt. To discern between good and evil.

We grow, we know the difference and seek a better outcome after our experience.

Making the right choices is vital to happiness.

Eve showed an example of trust.

Knowing the commandments her trust in God the Father and Redeemer Jesus Christ allowed for such mercy and testimony of true repentance.

Change, and trust in a divine intervention. Eve showed grace as it was given to her and Adam. Both partaking of the better path. Following God the Father and walking and talking with deity.

Such was the faith of this couple and Eve makes us feel humble as a chosen daughter of God was Eve.

And no doubt Eve gave us a profound gift of the right to choose- as stated by God the Father.

Mary

The woman honoured above all women

Scripture references-Matthew 1;2; 12-46; Luke1;2; John 2; 1-11; 19:25; Acts 1:14

Name meaning- No female has been honoured as has Mary by millions of peoples in all the world who have named their daughters Mary. This Hebrew name has ever been popular in all countries of the Western world and has altogether some twenty variations, the most conspicuous being Maria, Marie, Miriam and Miriamme. Mary is about the only feminine that has pronounced masculine forms such as Mario, Marion and Maria. Elsden C. Smith says that Mary heads the list of female names in America, the estimated number some ten years ago being 3,720,000 - Marie, 645,000- Marion, 444,000- Marian, 226,000. "The name Mary has been given at least 70 different interpretations in a frantic effort to get away from the Biblical significance of bitterness."

The name Mary occurs 51 times in the New Testament. and its prevalence there has been attributed to the popularity of Miriamne, the last representative of Hasmonean Family, who was the second wife of Herod I. As a name Mary is related to the Old Testament Miriam, to Mara, the name Naomi used to describe her affliction and to Mara the name of the bitter water reached by the Israelites in their wilderness journey's.

The original and pervading sense of these root-forms is that of "bitterness," derived from the notion of "trouble, sorrow, disobedience, rebellion."

Cruden gives "their rebellion" as the name-meaning of Miriam.

Mary the virgin, whom we are now considering, certainly had many "bitter" experiences as we shall see.

Family connections - According to the sacred record, Mary was a humble village woman who lived in a small town a place so insignificant as to lead Nathanael to say, "Can there anything good come out of Nazareth?"

(John 1:46), but out of it, and from the womb of the peasant woman came the greatest Man the world has ever known.

Mary was of the tribe of Judah, and the line of David. In the royal genealogy of Matthew and the human genealogy of Luke, Mary is only mentioned in the former, but her immediate forbears are not mentioned. She became the wife of Joseph, the son of Heli (Luke 3:23). Apart from Jesus, called her "firstborn", a term implied other children, followed after the order of natural generation (Luke 2:7). As a virgin, Mary bore Christ in a miraculous way, and Elisabeth most spontaneously and unaffectedly gave her the most honourable of titles, "Mother of the Lord" and praised her unstintedly as one "Blessed among women." Later Mary was married to Joseph the carpenter and she bore him four sons -James, Joses, Judas and Simon and the daughters unnamed. (Matthew 13:55,56; Mark 6:3). During his ministry none of his brothers believed in Him. Infact they sneered at Him and once concluded that He was mad, and wished to arrest Him and take Him away from Capernaum (Mark 21:21, 31, John 7:3-5) But as the result of His death and Resurrection, His brothers became believers, and were among the number gathered in the Upper Room before Pentecost. None of His brothers was apostle during His Lifetime. (Acts 1:13,14).

Mary as the mother of Jesus, is better known than any other female character in the Bible, and has been the best-known woman in the world since those days of the manger in Bethlehem.

After the century the statement still stands, "Blessed art thou among women" (Luke 1:28).

While we have no word as to her beauty or pedigree, we know that she was poor. Yet in the Bible and outside of it she came to occupy the highest place among women.

Lockyer H.(1996), The Women of the Bible page 92-93 Zondervan Publishing House, Michigan USA Holy Bible New International Version NIV

Mary (1) Mother of Jesus. The virgin, cousin of Elizabeth (Luke 1:36); betrothed to Joseph (Matt 1:18, Luke !: 27) the annunciation (26-38); visits Elizabeth (40-45); the Magnificat (46-55); returns (56;)

Joseph warned not to put her away, (Matt1:18-25); goes to Bethlehem with Joseph, (Luke 2:4-5); the nativity (7,16); visit of the shepherds (16-20); the Purification (2:21-38); the Magi visit (Matt 2:11); in Egypt

(13-14); returns to Nazareth (19-23; Luke 2:39); goes upto the Passover (41-52); at the wedding at Cana (John 2:2-5). Other references during the Lord's ministry include Matt 12: 46, 13 :54-55; Mark 3:21, 31; 6:3; Luke 8:19. She was entrusted to John (John 19: 25-26), and was with the Apostles after the ascension, (Acts 1:14). There is no trustworthy history of her later years. Latter day revelation confirms the biblical account and affirms that Mary was a pure and a chosen vessel, and the mother of the Son of God in the flesh (1 Nephi11: 13-20; Mosiah 3:8; Alma 7:10).

Reference: The Holy Bible AKJV (1989) Bible Dictionary Church of Jesus Christ of Latter- Day Saints Salt Lake City, Utah USA p. 729

Christian belief in Mary: Since Christians believe in a Virgin Birth (which Judaism does not accept) Jesus had no tribe (earthly father) so he cannot be considered to have a lineage of any tribe.

Matthew's gospel states the lineage as Jesus the adopted son of Joseph having been given status with the lineage of the House of David and the Tribe of Judah. If the lineage of Mary were to be considered; Mary being the earthly mother of Jesus and cousin of Elizabeth a Levite - Jesus had no lineage until adopted by Joseph in the Temple the eighth day after His birth by giving a sacrifice of two pidgeons. Thus paying, the price to adopt Jesus into the Tribe of Judah.

So, Jesus was known as Son of God and Son of David. During the time in which Christ was born, Judah was ruled by Rome. Had the Jews been free to Govern themselves, Joseph the Carpenter would have been crowned their King and Jesus would have been his rightful Heir. Thus, Jesus was literally King of the Jews. Fulfilling prophecy of old. Isaiah 9:6 Unto us a child is born. He will be the Prince of Peace.

As Jesus was from the Tribe of Judah as both Matthew1 and Luke 3 provide genealogies. This is in fulfillment of Jacob's prophecies for his 12 sons in Genesis 49. Judah is fourth in line.

Jesus, also called Jesus Christ, Jesus of Galilee, or Jesus of Nazareth, (born 6-4bc, Bethlehem- died c. ad 3, Jerusalem) religious leader revered in Christianity one of the world's major religions. He is regarded by most Christians as the incarnation of God. Incarnation meaning God became flesh.

Jesus | Facts, Teachings, Miracles & Doctrines | Brittanica

http://www.brittanica.com/biography/Jesus

SAINTS PROFILES

1. Saint Andrew

Andrew - Manliness.

Brother of Simon Peter, and one the twelve apostles (Matt. 4:18; 10:2).

The Man who was the First Missionary

Since he brought his own brother to the newly found Messiah, Andrew was recognised as the first missionary of Christ's cause (John 1:14). Andrew belonged to Bethsaida of Galilee. He was a follower of John the Baptist, who had a special bond with Christ (Mark 13:3; John 1:35-37). He was also fast at assisting (John 6:8, 9; 12:21,22). Andrew preached in Jerusalem, until the ascension of Jesus. Tradition has it that he was crucified for his rebuke of Aegeas for obstinate devotion to idolatry. He was nailed to the cross in the shape of an X, thus the term St. Andrew's Cross. Lessons to be learned from Andrew are:

I.   It is only in true discipleship that rest can be found.

II.   If we cannot perform more conspicuous service, we can yet serve the Lord. Although Peter was the spiritual father of the Pentecost converts, Andrew was their spiritual grandfather.

III. We must discover our own gift and the gift in others and guide such into right channels of service.

IV.   If we are Christ's ours will be the passion to lead others to Him.

2. Saint James

JAMES - supplanter.

The son of Zebedee, and the elder brother of John, and one of the Twelve (Matt. 4:21; 10:2; 17:1; Mark 1:19, 29; 3:17; 5:37; 9:2; 10:35; 41; 13:3; 14:33; Luke 5:10; 6:14; 8:51; 9:28, 54; Acts 1:13;12:2). From the Foregoing references several facts emerge:

James' father, Zebedee, was a prosperous Galilean fisherman and friend of the High Priest, Caiaphas. His mother was Salome, who was said to be the sister of the Virgin Mary, which would make him a cousin to Jesus.

James worked with his father and brothers and was busy with his boats and nets when Jesus asked him to follow him.

When the apostles set out two by two, James and John set out together and Jesus called them "Sons of Thunder."

His life came to an untimely end when he was martyred by Herod Agrippa. He served as an apostle for 17 years and he was the first to give his life for Christ.

We have no direct quotes from him, unless Acts 4:24-30 be and exception, but James was content to be a disciple.

3. Saint John

John- Jehovah hath been gracious.

John the son of Zebedee and Salome, the fishermen who became a beloved disciple, "the apostle of Love" The man whom Jesus loved.

John was the younger brother of James. He was a native of Bethsaida in Galilee. His parents were cousins of Christ and John was their youngest son. His father was prosperous. John himself was also a successful fisherman he was called to discipleship with his brother while working with his boats and nets. He was the youngest disciple of the Twelve. John, Peter and James were Christ's inner cabinet of three. Christ gave him the surname "Boanerges" because of his zeal and resolution to witness for Christ. He sat next to Christ at the Last Supper. He was instructed to look after Jesus's mother. His own mother followed Christ and anointed his body after the crucifixion. John nearly achieved the age of 100. He wrote the gospel and three epistles bearing his name as well as the Book of Revelation.

From references in the four gospels, Acts and Revelation, a preacher can determine the following traits in Johns character: his natural energy (Mark 3:17); his intolerance (Mark 9:38); his vindictiveness (Luke 9:54); his ambition (Mark 10:35-37); his eagerness to learn (John 13:23; I John 2:9); his sympathy (John 19:26); his love (I John 4:7-21).

4. Saint Jude

Jude- Praise.

Jude is the English form of the name Judas. He describes himself as a brother of James (Jude 1)

He was a brother to Jesus and like the rest of his brothers did not believe in Christ while they lived under the same roof (Matt. 13:55; John 7:5). His epistle appeals to the saints to defend the faith in an age of apostasy.

Jude's letter was addressed to a church or a circle of churches exposed to false teachers.

5. Saint Luke

Luke- light-giving or luminous.

The man who wrote the most beautiful book in the world. Not much is known of Luke, we do know he was a Gentile and probably the brother of Titus (II Cor. 8:16; 12:18). Paul speaks of him as a beloved Physician. Luke was a wealthy man, who was able to travel with Paul as a friend and useful companion (Acts 1:1; Col. 4:14; II Tim. 4:11; Philem. 24). Luke was a native of Antioch. He was a learned man, an exact observer and a faithful recorder. His medical training taught him to be exact. He is a reliable historian, scholar, skilful and sympathetic (Luke 1:1-3; Acts 1:1-3). His gospel is the most literary of the four. His writings followed the Greek style, they were studied and elaborate. As a poet, he was unsurpassed as a word-painter. Luke was inspired by the Holy Spirit for the ministry. Luke and Paul were close friends and Paul used Luke's gospel to preach. Luke's mission was to proclaim Christ's humanity. He traces Christ's lineage back to Adam and gives prominence to the sympathy and sociableness to Jesus as the Man (Luke 15:1) who came to save (Luke 19:10). Luke wrote both his gospel and the Book of Acts (Luke 1:1; Acts 1). And the characteristics of his gospel are:

Its graciousness – It's the gospel of pardon and redemption (Luke 1:28; 2:40).

Its sympathy - Christ is presented as the Healer of broken hearts and the Sharer of our woes. Luke is the gospel of philanthropy.

Its joyfulness - Angelic joy is prominent (Luke 1:14; 2:10,13; 15:7).

Its thanksgiving - The Church still sing these hymns written by Luke

Its teaching of the Holy Spirit. (Luke 1:15, 35, 41; 2:23, 26; 3:22; 4:1).

6. Saint Mark

Mark- A large hammer or polite.

He is known as the man who recovered himself.

Mark was the Roman surname of this apostle and his first name John, was his Hebrew name.

Mark was an apostle but not one of the original Twelve. John Mark was first mentioned in a prayer meeting held by his mother Mary at her house after Herod had just beheaded James and had Peter (The Big Fisherman) under arrest. These prayers were answered by the Lord (Acts 12:12). Mark's mother, Mary, was a well to do widow in Jerusalem and her house was often used as a meeting place for the saints (Acts 12:12; Col. 4:10). Her brother, Barnabas, was a healthy Levite from the island of Cyprus (Acts 13:1-5). Barnabas was a good friend and a counselor to Mark (Acts 11:24). Mark owes his conversion to Peter (I Pet 5:13). He became a close companion of Peter for 12 years. Mark is referred to as "the certain young man," who followed Christ when all His disciples forsook Him and fled (Mark 14:51).

Mark attended Paul and Barnabas when they set out on their great mission tour (Acts 13:5). In the early years Mark was guilty of vacillating (Acts 13:13; 15:38). Mark failed Paul and Barnabas in a difficult situation and divided the friends. The fear of difficulties on a missionary tour made Mark retrace his steps (Acts 13:13; 15:38). But later he became a valued colleague of Paul (Col. 4:10, 11; Philem. 24). Paul writes a tribute to Mark's usefulness (II Tim. 4:11). Peter too writes affectionately of Mark (I Pet 5:13). Mark became a bishop and a martyr, and he was buried in Venice. Saint Marks is dedicated to his memory. The Lion, the emblem of Mark's Roman Gospel, is emblazoned on the standard of the Venetian Republic. Because Mark's ministry was a Gentile one, he is recognised by his Gentile name. Writing specifically for Romans, who stood for power, Mark manifests Christ's power in service. Mark exhibited a soldier's rapid movements and gives us the shortest and simplest gospel. It is compact, direct, vivid and full of circumstantial evidence. The main lessons from Mark's life are:

I. The blessings of a godly home. The Christian Church owes much to Mary the mother of John Mark.

II. Much depends upon the choice of friends.

III. The possibilities of life. A widow's son became an apostle and a great historian.

IV. The reward for faithful service. Mark did not preach or perform miracles; he was known as the helper of others.

7. Saint Matthew

Matthew- The gift of Jehovah.

The man who left all to follow Christ.

This son of Alphaeus was a Hebrew with two names, often referred to as Levi, Levi means joined. Levi is the name he used when he was a tax collector (Luke 15:1) but he preferred Matthew when he joined the apostles. His original name connected him to the tribe of Levi. Matthew's new name, meaning the gift of God, emphasized the transforming power of Christ and indicated that Matthew was like the One who called him, a gift to Israel and to the world. His call to service came when he was sitting at the receipt of custom (Matt. 9:9; Luke 5:27) at Capernaum, the first world center, "the Great West Trunk Road from Damascus and the Far East to the Mediterranean Sea." Matthew was a "Publican" from the Latin word Publicannus, meaning collector of Roman taxes. The publicans reward was that he could extort for his own benefit more money than was due. As they gathered money for the Caesars they were pushed out of society and the Synagogue. "Jesus of Nazareth, the carpenter's son, knew Matthew the publican quite well," says Alexander Whyte. Jesus and his mother had moved to Capernaum. He had often been in Matthew's toll booth with his mother's taxes but when he called Matthew to serve as his disciple Matthew followed Christ without hesitation (Luke 5:28). To celebrate, Matthew entertained Christ and others to a feast in his own house (Matt. 9:10; Luke 5:29). Such a feast at home served a threefold purpose:

I.   It was Jubilee Feast to commemorate him moving into a new life.

II. It was a farewell dinner to publicly confess his surrender to the call of Christ.

III. It was a Conversazione to introduce his old friends and associates to his new found Saviour, that they too have an opportunity of hearing his wonderful words he knew many would come to his house to meet Christ who would not go to the Synagogue.

Matthew not only became an apostle but also the writer of the first gospel. Matthew gave us The Galilean Gospel. The only thing he took from his old life was his pen and ink. Matthew's gospel was the only one that gave us the Parables of the Kingdom the theme of his book was The King and His Kingdom he uses the word kingdom 56 times.

Matthew was well suited to commend Christ to the Jews. His gospel appeals to students of the Old Testament as a writer he is an eyewitness to the events he describes and an earwitness of the discourses he records. His book can be divided in this three-fold way:

The early days of the Messiah (Matt. 1-4:16)

The signs and works of the Messiah (Matt. 4:17-16:20)

The passion of the Messiah (Matt. 16:21- 28:20)

8. Saint Matthias

Matthias- Gift of God.

He is a disciple chosen by vote to succeed Judas Iscariot as an apostle. He had been a follower of Jesus from the beginning and was a witness of His resurrection (Acts 1:23, 26). Matthias was one of the 70 (Luke 10:1). David Smith feels that the choice of Matthias was not of God. The disciples prayed for guidance but instead of waiting for divine direction they casted votes. The election of Matthias was set aside, Paul becoming the successor of Judas. It is said that Matthias went to Ethiopia and laboured there and was ultimately martyred.

9. Saint Paul

Paul - Little.

The great apostle to the Gentiles, whose original name was Saul (Acts 13:9). The man who founded Churches.

Doctor John Clifford suggests that the making of this remarkable man is revealed in 6 photographs (see Acts 7:58; 22:3; 26:4,5; Rom. 7; Gal. 1:13, 15; Phil. 3:5, for these epochs).

I.   He was a native of Tarsus, and his father was a Roman (Acts 21:39; 22:3, 25; 25:16).

II.   He was a Pharisee Jew (Matt. 22:23; Acts 23:5, 6; Phil. 3:5).

III.   He was a free born citizen of Rome (Acts 22:25,28).

IV.   He had a strict religious training. Circumcision admitted him to the covenant relation of his fathers (Phil. 3:5). As a Jewish boy, he would memorise Scripture (Deut. 6:4-9) and familiarise himself with Jewish history (Deut. 6:20-25).

V.   He was a tent marker by trade (Acts 18:3). "What is commanded of a father towards his son? To circumcise him, to teach him the law, to teach him a trade" (see I Cor. 4:12; I Thess. 2:9; II Thess. 3:8).

VI.   He had received a good education, finishing up under the great philosopher Gamaliel (Acts. 22:3). Knowledge does not only come from books, but from the responsibility and experience of life. (Phil. 4:11-13).

VII.   He had been a persecutor of Christ and of Christians (Acts 8:1-4). Paul enthusiastically tried to stamp out the Christian faith. There is no evidence that he himself killed anyone.

VIII.   He became a news creature in Jesus Christ. The persecutor became a believer (Act 9:3-9; 22:6-11; 26:12-18).

IX. He had ten years training for this work in Arabia, Damascus, Jerusalem, Syria and Cilicia, Paul spent much time in the study of scriptures and in Prayer. (Gal. 1:15-24).

X. He was a great missionary and was a great church builder, he undertook three fruitful missionary journeys (Acts 13:1; 28:31). Paul was motivated by - "To do the will of Him that sent me" (John. 6:38; Acts 21:13, 14).

XI. He was a heart stirring preacher, ponder his sermon to Jews at Antioch (Acts 13:16-41); His sermon to Gentiles at Athens (Acts 17:22-31).

XII. He was a most gifted writer. Paul was the author of 14 of the 27 books of the New Testaments if we include Hebrews. Paul is described as a man of little stature, partly bald with crooked legs, of vigorous physique, with eyes set close together and a nose that is somewhat hooked. At the end of his life he was led out to the Appian Way where they cut his head from his frail body and he died triumphantly for the Lord.

10. Saint Peter

Peter - A rock or Stone.

The Greek of the Aramaic surname, Cephas. Peter was the brother of Andrew and the son of Jona, or Johanan (Matt. 4:18; John 1:40; I Cor. 1;12). The man that fell but rose again.

He was a fisherman of Bethsaida, a name meaning "the house of fish" and afterwards Capernaum. Peter and Andrew were both fishermen on the Lake of Galilee and were in partnership with Zebedee and his sons. Peter first met Christ at Bethany, where John the Baptist held his ministry. Both Peter and Andrew were disciples of the Baptist. Peter was a man with many facets of character. He was naturally impulsive (Matt. 14:28; 17:4; John. 21:7); tender-hearted and affectionate (Matt. 26:75; John 13:9; 21:15-17); gifted with spiritual insight (John 6:68), yet sometimes slow to apprehend deeper truths (Matt. 15:15,16); courageous in his confession of faith in Christ, yet guilty of a most cowardly denial (Matt. 16:16; John 6:69; Mark 14:67-71); self-sacrificing yet inclined towards self-seeking, (Matt. 19:27), and presumption (Matt. 16:22; John 13:8; 18:10); immovable in his convictions (Acts 4:19, 20; 5:28,29,40,42).

He became the leader and spokesman of the Twelve and of the three to witness the raising of Jairus` daughter and our Lord's agony in the garden. He became a miracle worker.

He made a confession of Christ's Deity which became the foundation of the Church. He denied Christ in his hour of need, yet he was restored by Jesus after His resurrection. After Pentecost, Peters' ministry appears in four stages:

I. Jerusalem activities, 29-35AD, when James succeeded to leadership of the Church.

II. Palestinian mission, 35-44AD, during which he stayed at Lydda and Joppa. He received a call to Caesarea.

III. Syrian mission with Antioch as a center, 44-61AD, during which he was accompanied by his wife, who became the pioneer Zenana missionary.

IV. Rome, 61AD, Peter arrived here before Paul's release from prison, and a few years later suffered martyrdom by crucifixion as Christ prophesied. Legend has it that Peter was crucified upside down.

11. Saint Philip

Philip - A warrior or a lover of horses.

Philip was one of the Twelve apostles and a native of Bethsaida in Galilee (Matt. 10:3; Mark 3:13). When asked by Jesus to become his disciple he asked if he may first bury his father (Matt. 8:21,22). The man of a timid retiring disposition.

Unlike Andrew and John, Philip did not approach Jesus but waited to be invited to join his company. Philip is his Greek name, but his Hebrew name is unknown.

In three lists Philip is bracketed with Nathanael as companion and fellow worker. The conversion and call of Philip are expressed simply: "Jesus...findeth Philip, and saith unto him, Follow me" (John 1:43). Right after his conversion Philip started bringing others to Christ. The convert became a soul winner.

When the hungry multitude gathered around Christ at the Sea of Galilee, Philip was tested by Christ (John 6:5). Philip fell short by declaring feeding the hungry masses was impossible. The seeking Greeks were led to Philip with their request to see Christ, he was afraid and almost lost an opportunity (John 12:21). Philip was slow to apprehend truth, he missed much, but Jesus had nothing but kind words for him (John 14:8). Philip died as a Martyr at Heirapolis.

12. Saint Thomas

Thomas - Twin.

He was also called Didymus (Matt.10:3; Mark 3:18; Luke 6:15; John 11:16; 14:5; 20:24-29; 21-2; Acts 1:13) The man who doubted.

Thomas was not really a name but an epithet, meaning, like its Greek equivalent Didymus, the twin. David Smith suggests that the apostle's name was Judas but that he was named the twin to distinguish him from Judas the son of James, and Judas Iscariot. Thomas wrote a gospel which is included in apocryphal literature.

He became known as 'Thomas the Doubter' after he was hesitant to accept the disciples' story of the Resurrection of Christ. Through the centuries Thomas was believed to be a typical pessimist and sceptic, the name Didymus hints at his propensity to doubt as some versions of the name mean double minded. Only John records Thomas in his gospel. Thomas is thought to have died a martyr. John describes three standout traits of Thomas:

I.   When he saw what needed to be done nothing kept him back. When Jesus expressed his intention of going into Judea, Thomas urged the disciples to company Christ even though it might mean death (John 11:16).

II.   When he saw what he ought to do, he only wanted to see how he was to do it. At the Last Supper he acknowledged his ignorance of the place his Lord was going to and asked how he could know the way (John 14:5).

III. When he saw what is was that he had to believe, he only wanted to see that it was right, and then to him there was no help for it. After our Lord's Resurrection, Thomas refused to believe in its reality expect upon conditions which he himself laid down - how stirring was his confession of faith once convinced of the Resurrection (John 20:28; 21:22).

13. Saint Timothy

Timothy- Honoured of God, worshiping of God, or Valued of God.

A young man of Lystra, son of Eunice, a Jewess by a Greek father who was probably dead when Paul visited the home (Act 16:1). The man who confessed a good confession.

How Paul describes Timothy:

I.   He was the child of Godly heritage (II Tim. 1:5) His mother was a Christian Jewess and the daughter of Lois another devout Jewess. His Greek father's name is unknown.

II. He was a youthful reader of scripture (II Tim. 3:15).

III. He was Paul's child in faith (I Cor. 4:17; I Tim. 1:2; II Tim. 1:2) Paul led Timothy to Christ during his ministry in Iconium and Lystra since he refers to his persecution there, which Timothy knew about (II Tim. 3:10, 11). One writer suggests that Paul recovered from his stoning at Lystra in Timothy's house.

IV. He was ordained a minister of the Gospel (I Tim. 4:14; II Tim. 1:6,7). Conscious of Timothy's unique gifts especially Evangelism (Rom. 16:21; II Tim. 4:5), Paul chose him as a companion and fellow worker. He served Paul faithfully, "as a son with his father", in spreading of the Gospel (Phil. 2:22). He became indispensable to Paul (Acts 17:14, 15; 18:5; 20:4) Paul and Timothy were like minded and Timothy enjoyed Paul's constant instruction (II Tim. 2:3; 3:14).

V.   Timothy was charged with difficult tasks like the responsibility of restoring a back sliding Church, these required both gift and grace (I Cor. 14:17), as did the comfort of believers in the middle of tribulation (I Thess. 3:2).

VI. He was co-sufferer with Paul in the afflictions of the Gospel (II Tim. 1:8). Timothy is said to have died as a martyr, as a bishop, in the reign of Domitian or Nerva. While attempting to stop an indecent heathen procession during the festival of Diana. The two epistles Paul addressed to Timothy are rich in counsel.

Bibliography

Lockyer, H. 1996, All The Men of The Bible

Zondervan Publishing House, Grand Rapids, Michigan USA

A Division of HarperCollins publishers Holy Bible New International Versoin NIV

With reference the following pages:

- Saint Andrew Pg. 49
- Saint James Pg. 169
- Saint John Pg. 196
- Saint Jude Pg. 211
- Saint Luke Pg. 220
- Saint Mark Pg. 229
- Saint Matthew Pg. 231
- Saint Matthias Pg. 233
- Saint Paul Pg. 269
- Saint Peter Pg. 272
- Saint Philip Pg. 276
- Saint Thomas Pg. 327
- Saint Timothy Pg. 329

THE SAINTS

Saint Andrew

Saint Thomas

Saint James

Saint Peter

SONGS

Love of My Life

Love i surrendour, remember

Love of my life

Love November, December

Our love in splendour

Love of my life

Love love you, love of my life

With this love i tremble

Love of my life

Your love is genuine

I shake, i wake to the sound

Of the love of my life

Lets dance while we can

As the nights will be day an

We will sigh as we in

Ways eternal love shines

Love of my life

Love of my life

Love of my life

Iiiiiiii love of my life

Lets dance, let the music take our romance

Iiiiiiilove of my life

Lets move to the music and sway through love of my life

Iiiiiiilove of my life

Love of my life

Love of my life

Love this life

With you iiiiiiilove of my life

Birthday Song

Birthdays are special

You are on the earth

So many years and more

There are many gifts

meanings more than material

kindness and hugs

and thankyou's

for a new day

even the best day

you receive goodness

the gestures of kindness

a fondness caress

the sight of all in formal dress

the party has started

no one is parted

all have greetings

many seatings

the ones gone

and close to the heart

counting blessings, the cake

presents, the phone will ring

all do sing

so it's happy birthday to you

happy birthday to you

and you blow out the candles one by one

for that someone close to you

The Songwriter

Take a flight and step into the wonder

I am the songwriter

from a corner of darkness to brightness

I have the power to change your life

I have the power to surprise and inspire

My words are like electricity to the soul

I sing life into your world

I am the songwriter

From a corner of darkness to lighting

up your world

Your faith I will inspire

I am the songwriter

Step into the wonder of music

flows like a river in your mind

the gold and silver in vision

Heaven is closer I am the songwriter

I am the songwriter I bring

strength and wisdom

completeness and rest

I am the songwriter

The Beloved

The beloved in the beginning

Bells wonderfully ringing

The love of the beloved

From stars, moon and suns

The love of the beloved

trailing glory in heaven above

Love of the beloved

Gave us life by a dove

We love the beloved

A star from afar

David's glory and story

The beloved in the begin

Mary mother of the Son

Of God the beloved

WE sing, sing we sing

Bells wonderfully ring

Trailing glory, we tell the story

The beloved in the beginning

Choirs enjoy singing

The beloved is come

The beloved is come

I'm Really Sorry

I'm really sorry

I'm really sorry

It happened that way

It happened that day

I didnt say

I'm really Sorry

I got away and i didnt say

I'm really sorry

You took it that way

Oh no Oh no

I am still your beau

Do you hear what i'm saying

I'm singing

I'm really sorry

I'm really sorry

Repeat the above 3 times

And sing

I'm okay now cause you still love me

Peace in Me

Peace in me, Peace in me

Peace is worth it

To calm the seas

Peace in me, peace in me

Peace be with you

Not of the world

But beyond the view

Be at peace

Peace in me

His life, my life, your life

No strife Its a matter of trust

Peace is a must

In this life, my life, your life

Peace in me

Be strong, no wrongs

Be at peace, with me, you and yours

Forevermore forevermore

Peace in Me

Calm the seas. with peace in me

and peace in our world

Sing I am Strong

Sing I am Strong

Sing I am Strong

Sing it loud and long

What makes us

And will not break us

Sing I am Strong

The call is one song

Sing I am Strong

Life and heart beat

This is so sweet

Sing I am Strong

Sing it with me

Ring the bells

Sing and sail on

Sing I am with thee

Sing your song

I am Stronger with thee

Time is us together

In all weather

Sing I am Strong

Strong

Strong

Strong with Thee

Look to the Heavens

Look to the heavens

I will be there

Yeah in your dreams

And heavenly prayers

Look to the heavens for me

And see the work unfold

You have been told

I will return you will discern

Look to the heavens and be

Exhalted in thee

Twinkling of an eye

It is me the only one

Believe and see me

In the heavens, sunset

Sunrise and open your eyes

Me in the heavens.

Life, Heart and My Soul

Life, heart and my soul

Life, heart and my soul

Life gave me a role

Life, heart and my soul

Heart felt good and moved my soul

My soul reach was my goal

Life gave me a role

Life, heart and my soul

In the beginning i see belief

In the end i know

There is a rainbow

For life, heart and my soul

The river of life is flowing

With the power of knowing

Jesus is coming to gather

Life, heart and my soul

In this life

In this life

Life.

Sons and Fathers

Sons and fathers with heart

turn to God on high

Sons and fathers

of the most high God

Sons and fathers with mind

remember to be kind

Sons and fathers

And listen to your God

Sons and fathers who love

to sing with choirs above

Sons and fathers

rejoice with your God

Sons and fathers Hear ye Him

Make joy in each hymn

Preach and turn the Fathers

to the children

Sons and fathers in similitude

Of the most high God

Teach and pray the children's

hearts turn to the fathers

Sons and fathers of the most high God

Horses

Walking, striding and colliding
With earth, shock to the brain
Now I sit in disdain
No fire burns, cold looks
I am searching for home
I ride a horse, it strides too
fast, I crash, horse reacts
kisses my cheek, yes I am
nursed and I no longer rehearse
I thnk, it's too late but i don't
feel distressed when doctor says
undress and checks for every
broken bone, or spinal pain
My head and pain going right down

my side. I lay flat face to sky
I pray, Oh God hear me 'no
broken bones' I say, Doctor Holmes will
not pay. I stay still, waiting no
relief. Girls gone except one who
cries, 'am I dead?. No I awake
walk to sit on log. I walk back
overcome. No report, I was too
sick to complain
. Did I slide,
did I cry, did I kick did
I not learn just to pace back
home. Each horse knew its course,
I was foolish, I risked my life.

Love lasts forever

Love lasts forever

Love is the treasure

Give it to someone

A n d care

Share your love to the one

There is a heaven

Love lasts forever

When one is touched

By the Word love

It is spiritual connection

A resurrection

Love lasts forever

Sense the moments

Get closer to treasure

The lasting love

Of Godly parents above

Love is the closest thing

To heaven sing

Love lasts forever

Love lasts

It is a treasure

And God created us as the treasure.

Life Brought Me to You

Life, living and loving is true

Life, loving with no blues

Life brought me to you

I thought I knew you

Before Life

Now we live life together

Through all weather

Better or Worse

Life is a force

Life brought me to you

Life, living and loving is true

Life, loving with no blues

And I am changing too

Because I met you

Help me make it forever

You are the treasure

Life brought me to you

Life, living and loving is true

Life with you is blest

Life is the best with you

Thank you

Thank you

Thank you

Strong Generation

https://youtu.be/hs-_srMyNUH

Door of Hope

https://youtu.be/4-iVIaCkqbY

Look to the Heavens

https://youtu.be/GunxG5NItBIw

Life, Heart and My Soul

https://www.youtube.com/watch?v=boE-IEqiUfY

connect with ldsradiostation.com

Printed in the United States
by Baker & Taylor Publisher Services